Mastering 11+
Cloze
Practice Book 1

Mastering 11+ © 2014 ashkraft educational

This page is intentionally left blank

Mastering 11+
Cloze
Exercice Book 1

Copyright © 2014 ASHKRAFT EDUCATIONAL

All rights reserved.

THIS PUBLICATION AND ITS CONTENTS ARE STRICTLY COPYRIGHT TO THE ASHKRAFT EDUCATIONAL. ANY UNAUTHORISED REPRODUCTION, MODIFICATION, DISTRIBUTION, DISPLAY, TRANSMISSION OR PUBLICATION OF THIS PAPER OR ANY CONTENT CONTAINED HEREIN IS ILLEGAL AND IS EXPRESSLY PROHIBITED

ASHKRAFT EDUCATIONAL HAS NO ASSOCIATION WITH
CEM, DURHAM UNIVERSITY, GL, ANY SCHOOL OR EXAMINATION BOARDS.

ISBN: 1502585499
ISBN-13: 978-1502585493

Exercises	Reference (From The Project Gutenberg EBooks)
1, 2, 3, 4 and 5	Little women by Louisa May Alcott
6, 7, 8, 9 and 10	The Lost Prince by Frances Hodgson Burnett
11, 12, 13, 14, 15, 16	Through The Looking-Glass by Lewis Caroll
17, 18, 19, 20	The Brownies and Other Tales by J.H.G. Ewing
21, 22, 23, 24, 25, 26, 27	Majorie's Three Gifts by Louisa M Alcott
28, 29, 30	Jo's boys by Luisa M Alcott

Every effort has been made to respect the copyright of the respective owners.
Please contact us in the first instance, if there are any queries with regards to copyrights of the contents of this bok.

DEDICATION

To all children preparing for the eleven plus exams and the parents who want nothing but the best for their kids.

> "I will prepare and some day my chance will come."
>
> Abraham Lincoln

Table of Contents

TYPE 1: MATCHING WORDS	1
CLOZE EXERCISE 1:	2
CLOZE EXERCISE 2:	5
CLOZE EXERCISE 3:	8
CLOZE EXERCISE 4:	11
CLOZE EXERCISE 5:	14
CLOZE EXERCISE 6:	17
CLOZE EXERCISE 7:	20
CLOZE EXERCISE 8:	23
CLOZE EXERCISE 9:	26
CLOZE EXERCISE 10:	29
CLOZE EXERCISE 11:	32
CLOZE EXERCISE 12:	35
CLOZE EXERCISE 13:	38
CLOZE EXERCISE 14:	41
CLOZE EXERCISE 15:	44
CLOZE EXERCISE 16:	47
CLOZE EXERCISE 17:	50
CLOZE EXERCISE 18:	53
CLOZE EXERCISE 19:	56
CLOZE EXERCISE 20:	59
TYPE 2: MULTIPLE CHOICE	62
CLOZE EXERCISE 21:	63
CLOZE EXERCISE 22:	66

CLOZE EXERCISE 23:	69
CLOZE EXERCISE 24:	72
CLOZE EXERCISE 25:	75
CLOZE EXERCISE 26:	78
CLOZE EXERCISE 27:	81
CLOZE EXERCISE 28:	84
CLOZE EXERCISE 29:	87
CLOZE EXERCISE 30:	90
ANSWERS	93

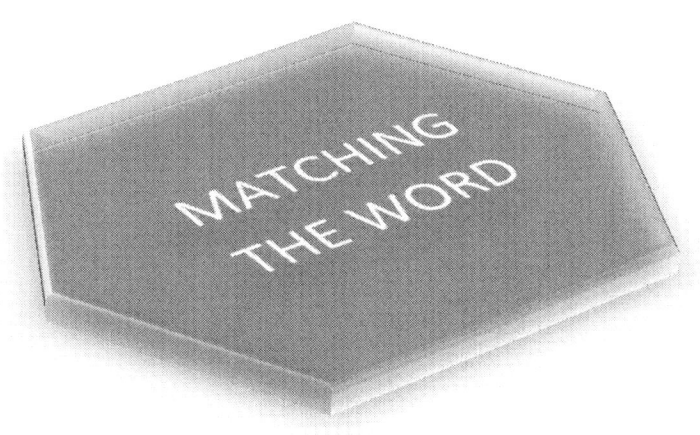

EXERCISE 1:

Instructions: For each question in the following passage, select the most appropriate word from the table below.

A. lived	B. books	C. sisters	D. because	E. table
F. coming	G. once	H. dawn	I. given	J. pillow

Jo was the first to wake in the gray [1] of Christmas morning. No stockings hung at the fireplace, and for a moment she felt as much disappointed as she did long ago, when her little sock fell down [2] it was crammed so full of goodies. Then she remembered her mother's promise and, slipping her hand under her pillow, drew out a little crimson-covered book. She knew it very well, for it was that beautiful old story of the best life ever [3] and Jo felt that it was a true guidebook for any pilgrim going on a long journey. She woke Meg with a "Merry Christmas," and bade her see what was under her [4] . A green-covered book appeared, with the same picture inside, and a few words written by their mother, which made their one present very precious in their eyes. Presently Beth and

Amy woke to rummage and find their little [5   ] also, one dove-colored, the other blue, and all sat looking at and talking about them, while the east grew rosy with the [6   ] day.

In spite of her small vanities, Margaret had a sweet and pious nature, which unconsciously influenced her [7   ], especially Jo, who loved her very tenderly, and obeyed her because her advice was so gently [8   ]

"Girls," said Meg seriously, looking from the tumbled head beside her to the two little night-capped ones in the room beyond, "Mother wants us to read and love and mind these books, and we must begin at [9   ]. We used to be faithful about it, but since Father went away and all this war trouble unsettled us, we have neglected many things. You can do as you please, but I shall keep my book on the [10   ] here and read a little every morning as soon as I wake, for I know it will do me good and help me through the day."

Exercise 1 - Answer Sheet:

	A	B	C	D	E	F	G	H	I
1	☐	☐	☐	☐	☐	☐	☐	☐	☐
2	☐	☐	☐	☐	☐	☐	☐	☐	☐
3	☐	☐	☐	☐	☐	☐	☐	☐	☐
4	☐	☐	☐	☐	☐	☐	☐	☐	☐
5	☐	☐	☐	☐	☐	☐	☐	☐	☐
6	☐	☐	☐	☐	☐	☐	☐	☐	☐
7	☐	☐	☐	☐	☐	☐	☐	☐	☐
8	☐	☐	☐	☐	☐	☐	☐	☐	☐
9	☐	☐	☐	☐	☐	☐	☐	☐	☐
10	☐	☐	☐	☐	☐	☐	☐	☐	☐

EXERCISE 2:

Instructions: For each question in the following passage, select the most appropriate word from the table below.

A. face	B. later	C. produced	D. friend	E. impressed
F. understand	G. soon	H. read	I. Christmas	J. stiffness

Then she opened her new book and began to [1]. Jo put her arm round her and, leaning cheek to cheek, read also, with the quiet expression so seldom seen on her restless [2].

"How good Meg is! Come, Amy, let's do as they do. I'll help you with the hard words, and they'll explain things if we don't [3]," whispered Beth, very much [4] by the pretty books and her sisters' example.

"I'm glad mine is blue," said Amy. and then the rooms were very still while the pages were softly turned, and the winter sunshine crept in to touch the bright heads and serious faces with a [5] greeting.

"Where is Mother?" asked Meg, as she and Jo ran down to thank her for their gifts, half an hour [6].

"Goodness only knows. Some poor creeter came a-beggin', and your ma went straight off to see what was needed. There never was such a woman for givin' away vittles and drink, clothes and firin'," replied Hannah, who had lived with the family since Meg was born, and was considered by them all more as a [7] than a servant.

"She will be back [8], I think, so fry your cakes, and have everything ready," said Meg, looking over the presents which were collected in a basket and kept under the sofa, ready to be [9] at the proper time. "Why, where is Amy's bottle of cologne?" she added, as the little flask did not appear.

"She took it out a minute ago, and went off with it to put a ribbon on it, or some such notion," replied Jo, dancing about the room to take the first [10] off the new army slippers.

Exercise 2 - Answer Sheet:

	A	B	C	D	E	F	G	H	I
1	▢	▢	▢	▢	▢	▢	▢	▢	▢
2	▢	▢	▢	▢	▢	▢	▢	▢	▢
3	▢	▢	▢	▢	▢	▢	▢	▢	▢
4	▢	▢	▢	▢	▢	▢	▢	▢	▢
5	▢	▢	▢	▢	▢	▢	▢	▢	▢
6	▢	▢	▢	▢	▢	▢	▢	▢	▢
7	▢	▢	▢	▢	▢	▢	▢	▢	▢
8	▢	▢	▢	▢	▢	▢	▢	▢	▢
9	▢	▢	▢	▢	▢	▢	▢	▢	▢
10	▢	▢	▢	▢	▢	▢	▢	▢	▢

EXERCISE 3:

Instructions: For each question in the following passage, select the most appropriate word from the table below.

A. burning	B. banished	C. defied	D. universal	E. Leaned
F. murmured	G. speech	H. serenade	I. gracefully	J. invited

A good deal of hammering went on before the curtain rose again, but when it became evident what a masterpiece of stage carpentry had been got up, no one [1] at the delay. It was truly superb. A tower rose to the ceiling, halfway up appeared a window with a lamp [2] in it, and behind the white curtain appeared Zara in a lovely blue and silver dress, waiting for Roderigo. He came in gorgeous array, with plumed cap, red cloak, chestnut lovelocks, a guitar, and the boots, of course. Kneeling at the foot of the tower, he sang a [3] in melting tones. Zara replied and, after a musical dialogue, consented to fly. Then came the grand effect of the play. Roderigo produced a rope ladder, with five steps to it, threw up one end, and [4] Zara to descend. Timidly she crept from her lattice, put her hand on Roderigo's shoulder, and was about to leap [5] down when "Alas! Alas for Zara!" she forgot her train. It caught in the window, the tower tottered, [6] forward, fell with a crash, and buried the unhappy lovers in the ruins.

A [7] shriek arose as the russet boots waved wildly from the wreck and a golden head emerged, exclaiming, "I told you so! I told you so!" With wonderful presence of mind, Don Pedro, the cruel sire, rushed in, dragged out his daughter, with a hasty aside...

"Don't laugh! Act as if it was all right!" and, ordering Roderigo up, [8] him from the kingdom with wrath and scorn. Though decidedly shaken by the fall from the tower upon him, Roderigo defied the old gentleman and refused to stir. This dauntless example fired Zara. She also [9] her sire, and he ordered them both to the deepest dungeons of the castle. A stout little retainer came in with chains and led them away, looking very much frightened and evidently forgetting the [10] he ought to have made.

Exercise 3 - Answer Sheet:

	A	B	C	D	E	F	G	H	I
1	☐	☐	☐	☐	☐	☐	☐	☐	☐
2	☐	☐	☐	☐	☐	☐	☐	☐	☐
3	☐	☐	☐	☐	☐	☐	☐	☐	☐
4	☐	☐	☐	☐	☐	☐	☐	☐	☐
5	☐	☐	☐	☐	☐	☐	☐	☐	☐
6	☐	☐	☐	☐	☐	☐	☐	☐	☐
7	☐	☐	☐	☐	☐	☐	☐	☐	☐
8	☐	☐	☐	☐	☐	☐	☐	☐	☐
9	☐	☐	☐	☐	☐	☐	☐	☐	☐
10	☐	☐	☐	☐	☐	☐	☐	☐	☐

EXERCISE 4:

Instructions: For each question in the following passage, select the most appropriate word from the table below.

A. now	B. heavier	C. Christmas	D. mind	E. shabby
F. pretty	G. Inclined	H. holidays	I. toil	J. work

"Oh, dear, how hard it does seem to take up our packs and go on," sighed Meg the morning after the party, for now the [1] were over, the week of merrymaking did not fit her for going on easily with the task she never liked.

"I wish it was [2] or New Year's all the time. Wouldn't it be fun?" answered Jo, yawning dismally.

"We shouldn't enjoy ourselves half so much as we do [3]. But it does seem so nice to have little suppers and bouquets, and go to parties, and drive home, and read and rest, and not [4]. It's like other people, you know, and I always envy girls who do such things, I'm so fond of luxury," said Meg, trying to decide which of two shabby gowns was the least [5].

"Well, we can't have it, so don't let us grumble but shoulder our bundles and trudge along as cheerfully as Marmee does. I'm sure Aunt March is a regular Old Man of the Sea to me, but I suppose when I've learned to carry her without complaining, she will tumble off, or get so light that I shan't [6] her."

This idea tickled Jo's fancy and put her in good spirits, but Meg didn't brighten, for her burden, consisting of four spoiled children, seemed [7] than ever. She had not heart enough even to make herself pretty as usual by putting on a blue neck ribbon and dressing her hair in the most becoming way.

"Where's the use of looking nice, when no one sees me but those cross midgets, and no one cares whether I'm [8] or not?" she muttered, shutting her drawer with a jerk. "I shall have to [9] and moil all my days, with only little bits of fun now and then, and get old and ugly and sour, because I'm poor and can't enjoy my life as other girls do. It's a shame!"

So Meg went down, wearing an injured look, and wasn't at all agreeable at breakfast time. Everyone seemed rather out of sorts and [10] to croak.

Exercise 4 - Answer Sheet:

	A	B	C	D	E	F	G	H	I
1	☐	☐	☐	☐	☐	☐	☐	☐	☐
2	☐	☐	☐	☐	☐	☐	☐	☐	☐
3	☐	☐	☐	☐	☐	☐	☐	☐	☐
4	☐	☐	☐	☐	☐	☐	☐	☐	☐
5	☐	☐	☐	☐	☐	☐	☐	☐	☐
6	☐	☐	☐	☐	☐	☐	☐	☐	☐
7	☐	☐	☐	☐	☐	☐	☐	☐	☐
8	☐	☐	☐	☐	☐	☐	☐	☐	☐
9	☐	☐	☐	☐	☐	☐	☐	☐	☐
10	☐	☐	☐	☐	☐	☐	☐	☐	☐

EXERCISE 5:

Instructions: For each question in the following passage, select the most appropriate word from the table below.

A. dearly	B. do	C. feeble	D. grateful	E. surprised
F. romance	G. changed	H. please	I. constantly	J. complaining

Mrs. March smiled and began at once, for she had told stories to this little audience for many years, and knew how to [1] them.

"Once upon a time, there were four girls, who had enough to eat and drink and wear, a good many comforts and pleasures, kind friends and parents who loved them [2] and yet they were not contented." (Here the listeners stole sly looks at one another, and began to sew diligently.) "These girls were anxious to be good and made many excellent resolutions, but they did not keep them very well, and were [3] saying, 'If only we had this,' or 'If we could only do that,' quite forgetting how much they already had, and how many things they actually could [4] . So they asked an old woman what spell they could use to make them happy, and she said, 'When you feel discontented, think over your blessings, and be [5] .'" (Here Jo looked up quickly, as if about to speak, but [6] her mind, seeing that the story was not done yet.)

"Being sensible girls, they decided to try her advice, and soon were [7] to see how well off they were. One discovered that money couldn't keep shame and sorrow out of rich people's houses, another that, though she was poor, she was a great deal happier, with her youth, health, and good spirits, than a certain fretful, [8] old lady who couldn't enjoy her comforts, a third that, disagreeable as it was to help get dinner, it was harder still to go begging for it and the fourth, that even carnelian rings were not so valuable as good behavior. So they agreed to stop [9] , to enjoy the blessings already possessed, and try to deserve them, lest they should be taken away entirely, instead of increased, and I believe they were never disappointed or sorry that they took the old woman's advice."

"Now, Marmee, that is very cunning of you to turn our own stories against us, and give us a sermon instead of a [10] !" cried Meg.

Exercise 5 - Answer Sheet:

	A	B	C	D	E	F	G	H	I
1	▭	▭	▭	▭	▭	▭	▭	▭	▭
2	▭	▭	▭	▭	▭	▭	▭	▭	▭
3	▭	▭	▭	▭	▭	▭	▭	▭	▭
4	▭	▭	▭	▭	▭	▭	▭	▭	▭
5	▭	▭	▭	▭	▭	▭	▭	▭	▭
6	▭	▭	▭	▭	▭	▭	▭	▭	▭
7	▭	▭	▭	▭	▭	▭	▭	▭	▭
8	▭	▭	▭	▭	▭	▭	▭	▭	▭
9	▭	▭	▭	▭	▭	▭	▭	▭	▭
10	▭	▭	▭	▭	▭	▭	▭	▭	▭

EXERCISE 6:

Instructions: For each question in the following passage, select the most appropriate word from the table below.

A. forgotten	B. dingier	C. basement	D. Intended	E. coming
F. furniture	G. alike	H. forlorn	I. remembered	J. railings

There are many dreary and dingy rows of ugly houses in certain parts of London, but there certainly could not be any row more ugly or [1] than Philibert Place. There were stories that it had once been more attractive, but that had been so long ago that no one [2] the time. It stood back in its gloomy, narrow strips of uncared-for, smoky gardens, whose broken iron [3] were supposed to protect it from the surging traffic of a road which was always roaring with the rattle of busses, cabs, drays, and vans, and the passing of people who were shabbily dressed and looked as if they were either going to hard work or [4] from it, or hurrying to see if they could find some of it to do to keep themselves from going hungry. The brick fronts of the houses were blackened with smoke, their windows were nearly all dirty and hung with dingy curtains, or had no curtains at all; the strips of ground, which had once been [5] to grow flowers in, had been trodden down into bare earth in which even weeds had [6] to grow. One of them was used as a stone-cutter's yard, and cheap monuments, crosses, and slates were set out for sale, bearing inscriptions beginning with "Sacred to the Memory of." Another had piles of old lumber in it, another exhibited second-hand [7], chairs with unsteady legs, sofas with horsehair stuffing bulging out of holes in their covering, mirrors with blotches or cracks in them. The insides of the houses were as gloomy as the outside. They were all exactly [8]. In each a dark entrance passage led to narrow stairs going up to bedrooms, and to narrow steps going down to a [9] kitchen. The back bedroom looked out on small, sooty, flagged yards, where thin cats quarreled, or sat on the coping of the brick walls hoping that sometime they might feel the sun; the front rooms looked over the noisy road, and through their windows came the roar and rattle of it. It was shabby and cheerless on the brightest days, and on foggy or rainy ones it was the most [10] place in London.

Exercise 6 - Answer Sheet:

	A	B	C	D	E	F	G	H	I
1	☐	☐	☐	☐	☐	☐	☐	☐	☐
2	☐	☐	☐	☐	☐	☐	☐	☐	☐
3	☐	☐	☐	☐	☐	☐	☐	☐	☐
4	☐	☐	☐	☐	☐	☐	☐	☐	☐
5	☐	☐	☐	☐	☐	☐	☐	☐	☐
6	☐	☐	☐	☐	☐	☐	☐	☐	☐
7	☐	☐	☐	☐	☐	☐	☐	☐	☐
8	☐	☐	☐	☐	☐	☐	☐	☐	☐
9	☐	☐	☐	☐	☐	☐	☐	☐	☐
10	☐	☐	☐	☐	☐	☐	☐	☐	☐

EXERCISE 7:

Instructions: For each question in the following passage, select the most appropriate word from the table below.

A. easily	B. more	C. do	D. aloof	E. changing
F. familiar	G. foreigner	H. taken	I. English	J. journeys

He had been in London [1] than once before, but not to the lodgings in Philibert Place. When he was brought a second or third time to a town or city, he always knew that the house he was [2] to would be in a quarter new to him, and he should not see again the people he had seen before. Such slight links of acquaintance as sometimes formed themselves between him and other children as shabby and poor as himself were [3] broken. His father, however, had never forbidden him to make chance acquaintances. He had, in fact, told him that he had reasons for not wishing him to hold himself [4] from other boys. The only barrier which must exist between them must be the barrier of silence concerning his wanderings from country to country. Other boys as poor as he was did not make constant [5], therefore they would miss nothing from his boyish talk when he omitted all mention of his.

When he was in Russia, he must speak only of Russian places and Russian people and customs. When he was in France, Germany, Austria, or England, he must [6] the same thing. When he had learned English, French, German, Italian, and Russian he did not know. He had seemed to grow up in the midst of [7] tongues which all seemed familiar to him, as languages are familiar to children who have lived with them until one scarcely seems less [8] than another. He did remember, however, that his father had always been unswerving in his attention to his pronunciation and method of speaking the language of any country they chanced to be living in.

"You must not seem a [9] in any country," he had said to him. "It is necessary that you should not. But when you are in England, you must not know French, or German, or anything but [10] ."

Once, when he was seven or eight years old, a boy had asked him what his father's work was.

"His own father is a carpenter, and he asked me if my father was one," Marco brought the story to Loristan.

Exercise 7 - Answer Sheet:

	A	B	C	D	E	F	G	H	I
1	☐	☐	☐	☐	☐	☐	☐	☐	☐
2	☐	☐	☐	☐	☐	☐	☐	☐	☐
3	☐	☐	☐	☐	☐	☐	☐	☐	☐
4	☐	☐	☐	☐	☐	☐	☐	☐	☐
5	☐	☐	☐	☐	☐	☐	☐	☐	☐
6	☐	☐	☐	☐	☐	☐	☐	☐	☐
7	☐	☐	☐	☐	☐	☐	☐	☐	☐
8	☐	☐	☐	☐	☐	☐	☐	☐	☐
9	☐	☐	☐	☐	☐	☐	☐	☐	☐
10	☐	☐	☐	☐	☐	☐	☐	☐	☐

EXERCISE 8:

Instructions: For each question in the following passage, select the most appropriate word from the table below.

A. envy	B. throne	C. chieftains	D. jealousies	E. tried
F. songs	G. tired	H. poorest	I. depose	J. poverty

In those past centuries, its people had been of such great stature, physical beauty, and strength, that they had been like a race of noble giants. They were in those days a pastoral people, whose rich crops and splendid flocks and herds were the [1] of less fertile countries. Among the shepherds and herdsmen there were poets who sang their own [2] when they piped among their sheep upon the mountain sides and in the flower-thick valleys. Their songs had been about patriotism and bravery, and faithfulness to their [3] and their country. The simple courtesy of the [4] peasant was as stately as the manner of a noble. But that, as Loristan had said with a tired smile, had been before they had had time to outlive and forget the Garden of Eden. Five hundred years ago, there had succeeded to the [5] a king who was bad and weak. His father had lived to be ninety years old, and his son had grown [6] of waiting in Samavia for his crown. He had gone out into the world, and visited other countries and their courts. When he returned and became king, he lived as no Samavian king had lived before. He was an extravagant, vicious man of furious temper and bitter [7]. He was jealous of the larger courts and countries he had seen, and [8] to introduce their customs and their ambitions. He ended by introducing their worst faults and vices. There arose political quarrels and savage new factions. Money was squandered until [9] began for the first time to stare the country in the face. The big Samavians, after their first stupefaction, broke forth into furious rage. There were mobs and riots, then bloody battles. Since it was the king who had worked this wrong, they would have none of him. They would [10] him and make his son king in his place.

Exercise 8 - Answer Sheet:

	A	B	C	D	E	F	G	H	I
1	☐	☐	☐	☐	☐	☐	☐	☐	☐
2	☐	☐	☐	☐	☐	☐	☐	☐	☐
3	☐	☐	☐	☐	☐	☐	☐	☐	☐
4	☐	☐	☐	☐	☐	☐	☐	☐	☐
5	☐	☐	☐	☐	☐	☐	☐	☐	☐
6	☐	☐	☐	☐	☐	☐	☐	☐	☐
7	☐	☐	☐	☐	☐	☐	☐	☐	☐
8	☐	☐	☐	☐	☐	☐	☐	☐	☐
9	☐	☐	☐	☐	☐	☐	☐	☐	☐
10	☐	☐	☐	☐	☐	☐	☐	☐	☐

EXERCISE 9:

Instructions: For each question in the following passage, select the most appropriate word from the table below.

| A. Rode | B. unlike | C. overpowered | D. shook | E. king |
| F. handsome | G. utterly | H. Herdsmen | I. private | J. himself |

The young prince was totally [1] his father. He was a true royal Samavian.

He was bigger and stronger for his age than any man in the country, and he was as [2] as a young Viking god. More than this, he had a lion's heart, and before he was sixteen, the shepherds and [3] had already begun to make songs about his young valor, and his kingly courtesy, and generous kindness. Not only the shepherds and herdsmen sang them, but the people in the streets. The king, his father, had always been jealous of him, even when he was only a beautiful, stately child whom the people roared with joy to see as he [4] through the streets. When he returned from his journeyings and found him a splendid youth, he detested him. When the people began to clamor and demand that he [5] should abdicate, he became insane with rage, and committed such cruelties that the people ran mad themselves.

One day they stormed the palace, killed and [6] the guards, and, rushing into the royal apartments, burst in upon the king as he shuddered green with terror and fury in his [7] room. He was king no more, and must leave the country, they vowed, as they closed round him with bared weapons and [8] them in his face. Where was the prince? They must see him and tell him their ultimatum. It was he whom they wanted for a [9] . They trusted him and would obey him. They began to shout aloud his name, calling him in a sort of chant in unison, "Prince Ivor—Prince Ivor—Prince Ivor!" But no answer came. The people of the palace had hidden themselves, and the place was [10] silent.

Exercise 9 - Answer Sheet:

	A	B	C	D	E	F	G	H	I
1	☐	☐	☐	☐	☐	☐	☐	☐	☐
2	☐	☐	☐	☐	☐	☐	☐	☐	☐
3	☐	☐	☐	☐	☐	☐	☐	☐	☐
4	☐	☐	☐	☐	☐	☐	☐	☐	☐
5	☐	☐	☐	☐	☐	☐	☐	☐	☐
6	☐	☐	☐	☐	☐	☐	☐	☐	☐
7	☐	☐	☐	☐	☐	☐	☐	☐	☐
8	☐	☐	☐	☐	☐	☐	☐	☐	☐
9	☐	☐	☐	☐	☐	☐	☐	☐	☐
10	☐	☐	☐	☐	☐	☐	☐	☐	☐

EXERCISE 10:

Instructions: For each question in the following passage, select the most appropriate word from the table below.

A. prisoner	B. mystery	C. assassinated	D. bone	E. return
F. fruitless	G. usele	H. searched	I. uprisings	J. beloved

In every nook and cranny, high and low, they sought for him, believing that the king himself had made him [1] in some secret place, or had privately had him killed. The fury of the people grew to frenzy. There were new risings, and every few days the palace was attacked and [2] again. But no trace of the prince was found. He had vanished as a star vanishes when it drops from its place in the sky. During a riot in the palace, when a last [3] search was made, the king himself was killed. A powerful noble who headed one of the [4] made himself king in his place. From that time, the once splendid little kingdom was like a [5] fought for by dogs. Its pastoral peace was forgotten. It was torn and worried and shaken by stronger countries. It tore and worried itself with internal fights. It [6] kings and created new ones. No man was sure in his youth what ruler his maturity would live under, or whether his children would die in [7] fights, or through stress of poverty and cruel, useless laws. There were no more shepherds and herdsmen who were poets, but on the mountain sides and in the valleys sometimes some of the old songs were sung. Those most [8] were songs about a Lost Prince whose name had been Ivor. If he had been king, he would have saved Samavia, the verses said, and all brave hearts believed that he would still [9] . In the modern cities, one of the jocular cynical sayings was, "Yes, that will happen when Prince Ivor comes again."

In his more childish days, Marco had been bitterly troubled by the unsolved [10] Where had he gone—the Lost Prince? Had he been killed, or had he been hidden away in a dungeon? But he was so big and brave, he would have broken out of any dungeon

Exercise 10 - Answer Sheet:

	A	B	C	D	E	F	G	H	I
1	☐	☐	☐	☐	☐	☐	☐	☐	☐
2	☐	☐	☐	☐	☐	☐	☐	☐	☐
3	☐	☐	☐	☐	☐	☐	☐	☐	☐
4	☐	☐	☐	☐	☐	☐	☐	☐	☐
5	☐	☐	☐	☐	☐	☐	☐	☐	☐
6	☐	☐	☐	☐	☐	☐	☐	☐	☐
7	☐	☐	☐	☐	☐	☐	☐	☐	☐
8	☐	☐	☐	☐	☐	☐	☐	☐	☐
9	☐	☐	☐	☐	☐	☐	☐	☐	☐
10	☐	☐	☐	☐	☐	☐	☐	☐	☐

EXERCISE 11:

Instructions: For each question in the following passage, select the most appropriate word from the table below.

| A. hand | B. touching | C. manners | D. earlier | E. tail |
| F. ball | G. rolling | H. white | I. manage | J. paw |

One thing was certain, that the WHITE kitten had had nothing to do with it:—it was the black kitten's fault entirely. For the [1] kitten had been having its face washed by the old cat for the last quarter of an hour (and bearing it pretty well, considering); so you see that it COULDN'T have had any [2] in the mischief.

The way Dinah washed her children's faces was this: first she held the poor thing down by its ear with one paw, and then with the other [3] she rubbed its face all over, the wrong way, beginning at the nose: and just now, as I said, she was hard at work on the white kitten, which was lying quite still and trying to purr—no doubt feeling that it was all meant for its good.

But the black kitten had been finished with [4] in the afternoon, and so, while Alice was sitting curled up in a corner of the great arm-chair, half talking to herself and half asleep, the kitten had been having a grand game of romps with the ball of worsted Alice had been trying to wind up, and had been [5] it up and down till it had all come undone again; and there it was, spread over the hearth-rug, all knots and tangles, with the kitten running after its own [6] in the middle.

'Oh, you wicked little thing!' cried Alice, catching up the kitten, and giving it a little kiss to make it understand that it was in disgrace. 'Really, Dinah ought to have taught you better [7]! You OUGHT, Dinah, you know you ought!' she added, looking reproachfully at the old cat, and speaking in as cross a voice as she could [8]—and then she scrambled back into the arm-chair, taking the kitten and the worsted with her, and began winding up the [9] again. But she didn't get on very fast, as she was talking all the time, sometimes to the kitten, and [10] to herself.

Exercise 11 - Answer Sheet:

	A	B	C	D	E	F	G	H	I
1	☐	☐	☐	☐	☐	☐	☐	☐	☐
2	☐	☐	☐	☐	☐	☐	☐	☐	☐
3	☐	☐	☐	☐	☐	☐	☐	☐	☐
4	☐	☐	☐	☐	☐	☐	☐	☐	☐
5	☐	☐	☐	☐	☐	☐	☐	☐	☐
6	☐	☐	☐	☐	☐	☐	☐	☐	☐
7	☐	☐	☐	☐	☐	☐	☐	☐	☐
8	☐	☐	☐	☐	☐	☐	☐	☐	☐
9	☐	☐	☐	☐	☐	☐	☐	☐	☐
10	☐	☐	☐	☐	☐	☐	☐	☐	☐

EXERCISE 12:

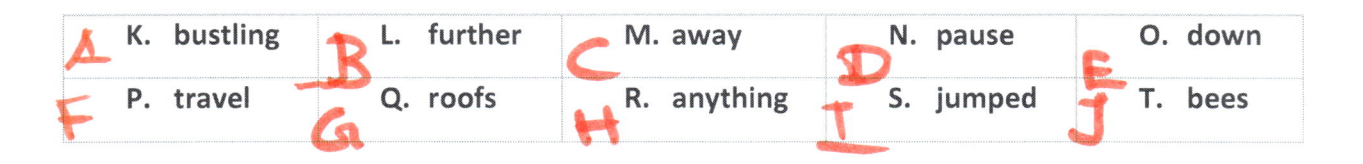

Instructions: For each question in the following passage, select the most appropriate word from the table below.

A / K. bustling	B / L. further	C / M. away	D / N. pause	E / O. down
F / P. travel	G / Q. roofs	H / R. anything	I / S. jumped	J / T. bees

Of course the first thing to do was to make a grand survey of the country she was going to

[1] through. 'It's something very like learning geography,' thought Alice,

as she stood on tiptoe in hopes of being able to see a little [2]. 'Principal

rivers—there ARE none. Principal mountains—I'm on the only one, but I don't think it's got

any name. Principal towns—why, what ARE those creatures, making honey down there?

They can't be bees—nobody ever saw [3] a mile off, you know—'

and for some time she stood silent, watching one of them that was [4]

about among the flowers, poking its proboscis into them, 'just as if it was a regular bee,'

thought Alice.

However, this was [5] but a regular bee: in fact it was an elephant—as

Page | 35   Mastering 11+/Close – Book ONE/ashkraft educational

Alice soon found out, though the idea quite took her breath [6] at first. 'And what enormous flowers they must be!' was her next idea. 'Something like cottages with the [7] taken off, and stalks put to them—and what quantities of honey they must make! I think I'll go down and—no, I won't JUST yet,' she went on, checking herself just as she was beginning to run [8] the hill, and trying to find some excuse for turning shy so suddenly. 'It'll never do to go down among them without a good long branch to brush them away—and what fun it'll be when they ask me how I like my walk. I shall say—"Oh, I like it well enough—"' (here came the favourite little toss of the head), '"only it was so dusty and hot, and the elephants did tease so!"'

'I think I'll go down the other way,' she said after a [9] : 'and perhaps I may visit the elephants later on. Besides, I do so want to get into the Third Square!'

So with this excuse she ran down the hill and [10] over the first of the six little brooks.

Exercise 12 - Answer Sheet:

	A	B	C	D	E	F	G	H	I
1	☐	☐	☐	☐	☐	☐	☐	☐	☐
2	☐	☐	☐	☐	☐	☐	☐	☐	☐
3	☐	☐	☐	☐	☐	☐	☐	☐	☐
4	☐	☐	☐	☐	☐	☐	☐	☐	☐
5	☐	☐	☐	☐	☐	☐	☐	☐	☐
6	☐	☐	☐	☐	☐	☐	☐	☐	☐
7	☐	☐	☐	☐	☐	☐	☐	☐	☐
8	☐	☐	☐	☐	☐	☐	☐	☐	☐
9	☐	☐	☐	☐	☐	☐	☐	☐	☐
10	☐	☐	☐	☐	☐	☐	☐	☐	☐

EXERCISE 13:

Instructions: For each question in the following passage, select the most appropriate word from the table below.

A. ticket	B. came	C. opposite	D. inch	E. bought
F. waiting	G. word	H. angrily	I. microscope	J. chorus

'Tickets, please!' said the Guard, putting his head in at the window. In a moment everybody was holding out a [1]: they were about the same size as the people, and quite seemed to fill the carriage. 'Now then! Show your ticket, child!' the Guard went on, looking [2] at Alice. And a great many voices all said together ('like the chorus of a song,' thought Alice), 'Don't keep him [3], child! Why, his time is worth a thousand pounds a minute!'

'I'm afraid I haven't got one,' Alice said in a frightened tone: 'there wasn't a ticket-office where I [4] from.' And again the chorus of voices went on. 'There wasn't room for one where she came from. The land there is worth a thousand pounds an [5]!'

'Don't make excuses,' said the Guard: 'you should have [6] one from the engine-driver.' And once more the [7] of voices went on with 'The man that drives the engine. Why, the smoke alone is worth a thousand pounds a puff!'

Alice thought to herself, 'Then there's no use in speaking.' The voices didn't join in this time, as she hadn't spoken, but to her great surprise, they all THOUGHT in chorus (I hope you understand what THINKING IN CHORUS means—for I must confess that I don't), 'Better say nothing at all. Language is worth a thousand pounds a [8] !'

'I shall dream about a thousand pounds tonight, I know I shall!' thought Alice.

All this time the Guard was looking at her, first through a telescope, then through a [9] , and then through an opera-glass. At last he said, 'You're travelling the wrong way,' and shut up the window and went away.

'So young a child,' said the gentleman sitting [10] to her (he was dressed in white paper), 'ought to know which way she's going, even if she doesn't know her own name!'

Exercise 13 - Answer Sheet:

	A	B	C	D	E	F	G	H	I
1	☐	☐	☐	☐	☐	☐	☐	☐	☐
2	☐	☐	☐	☐	☐	☐	☐	☐	☐
3	☐	☐	☐	☐	☐	☐	☐	☐	☐
4	☐	☐	☐	☐	☐	☐	☐	☐	☐
5	☐	☐	☐	☐	☐	☐	☐	☐	☐
6	☐	☐	☐	☐	☐	☐	☐	☐	☐
7	☐	☐	☐	☐	☐	☐	☐	☐	☐
8	☐	☐	☐	☐	☐	☐	☐	☐	☐
9	☐	☐	☐	☐	☐	☐	☐	☐	☐
10	☐	☐	☐	☐	☐	☐	☐	☐	☐

EXERCISE 14:

Instructions: For each question in the following passage, select the most appropriate word from the table below.

A. conversation	B. pinned	C. untidy	D. groaned	E. gently
F. meet	G. wildly	H. addressing	I. melancholy	J. shawl

She caught the shawl as she spoke, and looked about for the owner: in another moment the White Queen came running [1] through the wood, with both arms stretched out wide, as if she were flying, and Alice very civilly went to [2] her with the shawl. 'I'm very glad I happened to be in the way,' Alice said, as she helped her to put on her [3] again.

The White Queen only looked at her in a helpless frightened sort of way, and kept repeating something in a whisper to herself that sounded like 'bread-and-butter, bread-and-butter,' and Alice felt that if there was to be any [4] at all, she must manage it herself. So she began rather timidly: 'Am I [5] the White Queen?'

'Well, yes, if you call that a-dressing,' The Queen said. 'It isn't MY notion of the thing, at all.'

Alice thought it would never do to have an argument at the very beginning of their conversation, so she smiled and said, 'If your Majesty will only tell me the right way to begin, I'll do it as well as I can.'

'But I don't want it done at all!' [6] the poor Queen. 'I've been a-dressing myself for the last two hours.'

It would have been all the better, as it seemed to Alice, if she had got someone else to dress her, she was so dreadfully [7] . 'Every single thing's crooked,' Alice thought to herself, 'and she's all over pins!—may I put your shawl straight for you?' she added aloud.

'I don't know what's the matter with it!' the Queen said, in a [8] voice. 'It's out of temper, I think. I've pinned it here, and I've [9] it there, but there's no pleasing it!' 'It CAN'T go straight, you know, if you pin it all on one side,' Alice said, as she [10] put it right for her; 'and, dear me, what a state your hair is in!'

Exercise 14 - Answer Sheet:

	A	B	C	D	E	F	G	H	I
1	▭	▭	▭	▭	▭	▭	▭	▭	▭
2	▭	▭	▭	▭	▭	▭	▭	▭	▭
3	▭	▭	▭	▭	▭	▭	▭	▭	▭
4	▭	▭	▭	▭	▭	▭	▭	▭	▭
5	▭	▭	▭	▭	▭	▭	▭	▭	▭
6	▭	▭	▭	▭	▭	▭	▭	▭	▭
7	▭	▭	▭	▭	▭	▭	▭	▭	▭
8	▭	▭	▭	▭	▭	▭	▭	▭	▭
9	▭	▭	▭	▭	▭	▭	▭	▭	▭
10	▭	▭	▭	▭	▭	▭	▭	▭	▭

EXERCISE 15:

Instructions: For each question in the following passage, select the most appropriate word from the table below.

A. herself	B. legs	C. fall	D. mouth	E. looking
F. Stuffed	G. written	H. anything	I. evidently	J. compliment

However, the egg only got larger and larger, and more and more human: when she had come within a few yards of it, she saw that it had eyes and a nose and [1] ; and when she had come close to it, she saw clearly that it was HUMPTY DUMPTY himself. 'It can't be anybody else!' she said to [2]. 'I'm as certain of it, as if his name were [3] all over his face.'

It might have been written a hundred times, easily, on that enormous face. Humpty Dumpty was sitting with his [4] crossed, like a Turk, on the top of a high wall—such a narrow one that Alice quite wondered how he could keep his balance—and, as his eyes were steadily fixed in the opposite direction, and he didn't take the least notice of her, she thought he must be a [5] figure after all.

'And how exactly like an egg he is!' she said aloud, standing with her hands ready to catch him, for she was every moment expecting him to [6]   .

'It's VERY provoking,' Humpty Dumpty said after a long silence, looking away from Alice as he spoke, 'to be called an egg—VERY!'

'I said you LOOKED like an egg, Sir,' Alice gently explained. 'And some eggs are very pretty, you know' she added, hoping to turn her remark into a sort of a [7]   .

'Some people,' said Humpty Dumpty, [8]   away from her as usual, 'have no more sense than a baby!' Alice didn't know what to say to this: it wasn't at all like conversation, she thought, as he never said [9]   to HER; in fact, his last remark was [10]   addressed to a tree—so she stood and softly repeated to herself:—

'Humpty Dumpty sat on a wall:
Humpty Dumpty had a great fall.
All the King's horses and all the King's men
Couldn't put Humpty Dumpty in his place again.'

Exercise 15 - Answer Sheet:

	A	B	C	D	E	F	G	H	I
1	☐	☐	☐	☐	☐	☐	☐	☐	☐
2	☐	☐	☐	☐	☐	☐	☐	☐	☐
3	☐	☐	☐	☐	☐	☐	☐	☐	☐
4	☐	☐	☐	☐	☐	☐	☐	☐	☐
5	☐	☐	☐	☐	☐	☐	☐	☐	☐
6	☐	☐	☐	☐	☐	☐	☐	☐	☐
7	☐	☐	☐	☐	☐	☐	☐	☐	☐
8	☐	☐	☐	☐	☐	☐	☐	☐	☐
9	☐	☐	☐	☐	☐	☐	☐	☐	☐
10	☐	☐	☐	☐	☐	☐	☐	☐	☐

EXERCISE 16:

Instructions: For each question in the following passage, select the most appropriate word from the table below.

| A. soldiers | B. fear | C. exact | D. writing | E. woods |
| F. twenty | G. delight | H. stumbled | I. eyes | J. fell |

The next moment soldiers came running through the wood, at first in twos and threes, then ten or [1] together, and at last in such crowds that they seemed to fill the whole forest. Alice got behind a tree, for [2] of being run over, and watched them go by.

She thought that in all her life she had never seen [3] so uncertain on their feet: they were always tripping over something or other, and whenever one went down, several more always [4] over him, so that the ground was soon covered with little heaps of men.

Then came the horses. Having four feet, these managed rather better than the foot-soldiers: but even THEY [5] now and then; and it seemed to be a regular rule that, whenever a horse stumbled the rider fell off instantly. The confusion got worse every moment, and Alice was very glad to get out of the wood into an open place, where she found the White King seated on the ground, busily [6] in his memorandum-book.

'I've sent them all!' the King cried in a tone of [7], on seeing Alice. 'Did you happen to meet any soldiers, my dear, as you came through the [8]?'

'Yes, I did,' said Alice: 'several thousand, I should think.'

'Four thousand two hundred and seven, that's the [9] number,' the King said, referring to his book. 'I couldn't send all the horses, you know, because two of them are wanted in the game. And I haven't sent the two Messengers, either. They're both gone to the town. Just look along the road, and tell me if you can see either of them.'

'I see nobody on the road,' said Alice. 'I only wish I had such [10],' the King remarked in a fretful tone. 'To be able to see Nobody! And at that distance, too! Why, it's as much as I can do to see real people, by this light!'

Exercise 16 - Answer Sheet:

	A	B	C	D	E	F	G	H	I
1	☐	☐	☐	☐	☐	☐	☐	☐	☐
2	☐	☐	☐	☐	☐	☐	☐	☐	☐
3	☐	☐	☐	☐	☐	☐	☐	☐	☐
4	☐	☐	☐	☐	☐	☐	☐	☐	☐
5	☐	☐	☐	☐	☐	☐	☐	☐	☐
6	☐	☐	☐	☐	☐	☐	☐	☐	☐
7	☐	☐	☐	☐	☐	☐	☐	☐	☐
8	☐	☐	☐	☐	☐	☐	☐	☐	☐
9	☐	☐	☐	☐	☐	☐	☐	☐	☐
10	☐	☐	☐	☐	☐	☐	☐	☐	☐

EXERCISE 17:

Instructions: For each question in the following passage, select the most appropriate word from the table below.

| A. clearly | B. depressing | C. breeze | D. climbing | E. slim |
| F. help | G. pleased | H. thickening | I. wonderful | J. murmured |

A little girl sat sewing and crying on a garden seat. She had fair floating hair, which the

[1] blew into her eyes, and between the cloud of hair, and the mist of

tears, she could not see her work very [2]. She neither tied up her locks,

nor dried her eyes, however; for when one is miserable, one may as well be completely so.

"What is the matter?" said the Doctor, who was a friend of the Rector's, and came into the

garden whenever he [3] .

The Doctor was a tall stout man, with hair as black as crow's feathers on the top, and grey

underneath, and a bushy beard. When young, he had been [4] and

handsome, with wonderful eyes, which were [5] still; but that was many years past. He had a great love for children, and this one was a particular friend of his.

"What is the matter?" said he.

"I'm in a row," [6] the young lady through her veil; and the needle went in damp, and came out with a jerk, which is apt to result in what ladies called "puckering."

"You are like London in a yellow fog," said the Doctor, throwing himself on to the grass, "and it is very [7] to my feelings. What is the row about, and how came you to get into it?"

"We're all in it," was the reply; and apparently the fog was [8] , for the voice grew less and less distinct—"the boys and everybody. It's all about forgetting, and not putting away, and leaving about, and borrowing, and breaking, and that sort of thing. I've had Father's new pocket-handkerchiefs to hem, and I've been out [9] with the boys, and kept forgetting and forgetting, and Mother says I always forget; and I can't [10] it.

Exercise 17 - Answer Sheet:

	A	B	C	D	E	F	G	H	I
1	▢	▢	▢	▢	▢	▢	▢	▢	▢
2	▢	▢	▢	▢	▢	▢	▢	▢	▢
3	▢	▢	▢	▢	▢	▢	▢	▢	▢
4	▢	▢	▢	▢	▢	▢	▢	▢	▢
5	▢	▢	▢	▢	▢	▢	▢	▢	▢
6	▢	▢	▢	▢	▢	▢	▢	▢	▢
7	▢	▢	▢	▢	▢	▢	▢	▢	▢
8	▢	▢	▢	▢	▢	▢	▢	▢	▢
9	▢	▢	▢	▢	▢	▢	▢	▢	▢
10	▢	▢	▢	▢	▢	▢	▢	▢	▢

EXERCISE 18:

Instructions: For each question in the following passage, select the most appropriate word from the table below.

A. son	B. spoilt	C. troubles	D. intellect	E. tailoring
F. churchyard	G. England	H. grandchildren	I. children	J. memory

"Bairns are a burden," said the Tailor to himself as he sat at work. He lived in a village on some of the glorious moors of the north of [1] ; and by bairns he meant children, as every Northman knows.

"Bairns are a burden," and he sighed. "Bairns are a blessing," said the old lady in the window. "It is the family motto. The Trouts have had large families and good luck for generations; that is, till your grandfather's time. He had one only [2] . I married him. He was a good husband, but he had been a [3] child. He had always been used to be waited upon, and he couldn't fash to look after the farm when it was his own. We had six [4] . They are all dead but you, who were the youngest.

You were bound to a tailor. When the farm came into your hands, your wife died, and you have never looked up since. The land is sold now, but not the house. No! no! you're right enough there; but you've had your [5], son Thomas, and the lads are idle!"

It was the Tailor's mother who spoke. She was a very old woman, and helpless. She was not quite so bright in her [6] as she had been, and got muddled over things that had lately happened; but she had a clear [7] for what was long past, and was very pertinacious in her opinions. She knew the private history of almost every family in the place, and who of the Trouts were buried under which old stones in the [8]; and had more tales of ghosts, doubles, warnings, fairies, witches, hobgoblins, and such like, than even her [9] had ever come to the end of. Her hands trembled with age, and she regretted this for nothing more than for the danger it brought her into of spilling the salt. She was past housework, but all day she sat knitting hearth-rugs out of the bits and scraps of cloth that were shred in the [10].

Exercise 18 - Answer Sheet:

	A	B	C	D	E	F	G	H	I
1	☐	☐	☐	☐	☐	☐	☐	☐	☐
2	☐	☐	☐	☐	☐	☐	☐	☐	☐
3	☐	☐	☐	☐	☐	☐	☐	☐	☐
4	☐	☐	☐	☐	☐	☐	☐	☐	☐
5	☐	☐	☐	☐	☐	☐	☐	☐	☐
6	☐	☐	☐	☐	☐	☐	☐	☐	☐
7	☐	☐	☐	☐	☐	☐	☐	☐	☐
8	☐	☐	☐	☐	☐	☐	☐	☐	☐
9	☐	☐	☐	☐	☐	☐	☐	☐	☐
10	☐	☐	☐	☐	☐	☐	☐	☐	☐

EXERCISE 19:

Instructions: For each question in the following passage, select the most appropriate word from the table below.

| A. risen | B. before | C. somebody | D. examine | E. shadows |
| F. blinking | G. asleep | H. shuddered | I. like | J. down |

The moon rose like gold, and went up into the heavens like silver, flooding the moors with a pale ghostly light, taking the colour out of the heather, and painting black [1] under the stone walls. Tommy opened his eyes, and ran to the window. "The moon has [2] ," said he, and crept softly down the ladder, through the kitchen, where was the pan of water, but no Brownie, and so out on to the moor. The air was fresh, not to say chilly; but it was a glorious night, though everything but the wind and Tommy seemed [3] . The stones, the walls, the gleaming lanes, were so intensely still; the church tower in the valley seemed awake and watching, but silent; the houses in the village round it had all their eyes shut, that is, their window-blinds [4] ; and it seemed to Tommy as if the very moors had drawn white sheets over them, and lay sleeping also.

"Hoot! hoot!" said a voice from the fir plantation behind him. [5] else was awake, then. "It's the Old Owl," said Tommy; and there she came, swinging heavily across the moor with a flapping stately flight, and sailed into the shed by the mere. The old lady moved faster than she seemed to do, and though Tommy ran hard she was in the shed some time [6] him. When he got in, no bird was to be seen, but he heard a crunching sound from above, and looking up, there sat the Old Owl, pecking and tearing and munching at some shapeless black object, and [7] at him—Tommy—with yellow eyes.

"Oh dear!" said Tommy, for he didn't much [8] it.

The Old Owl dropped the black mass on to the floor; and Tommy did not care somehow to [9] it.

"Come up! come up!" said she hoarsely. She could speak, then! Beyond all doubt it was the Old Owl, and none other. Tommy [10] .

Exercise 19 - Answer Sheet:

	A	B	C	D	E	F	G	H	I
1	☐	☐	☐	☐	☐	☐	☐	☐	☐
2	☐	☐	☐	☐	☐	☐	☐	☐	☐
3	☐	☐	☐	☐	☐	☐	☐	☐	☐
4	☐	☐	☐	☐	☐	☐	☐	☐	☐
5	☐	☐	☐	☐	☐	☐	☐	☐	☐
6	☐	☐	☐	☐	☐	☐	☐	☐	☐
7	☐	☐	☐	☐	☐	☐	☐	☐	☐
8	☐	☐	☐	☐	☐	☐	☐	☐	☐
9	☐	☐	☐	☐	☐	☐	☐	☐	☐
10	☐	☐	☐	☐	☐	☐	☐	☐	☐

EXERCISE 20:

Instructions: For each question in the following passage, select the most appropriate word from the table below.

A. broke	B. saying	C. antidote	D. bedroom	E. further
F. unselfish	G. condemned	H. occasion	I. naughty	J. burst

It was certainly an aggravated offence. It is generally understood in families that "boys will be boys," but there is a limit to the forbearance implied in the extenuating axiom. Master Sam was [1] to the back nursery for the rest of the day.

He always had had the knack of breaking his own toys,—he not unfrequently [2] other people's; but accidents will happen, and his twin-sister and factotum, Dot, was long-suffering.

Dot was fat, resolute, hasty, and devotedly [3]. When Sam scalped her new doll, and fastened the glossy black curls to a wigwam improvised with the curtains of the four-post bed in the best [4], Dot was sorely tried. As her eyes passed from the crown-less doll on the floor to the floss-silk ringlets hanging from the bed-furniture, her round rosy face grew rounder and rosier, and tears [5] from her eyes. But in a moment more she clenched her little fists, forced back the tears, and gave vent to her favourite [6], "I don't care."

That sentence was Dot's bane and [7]; it was her vice and her virtue. It was her standing consolation, and it brought her into all her scrapes. It was her one panacea for all the ups and downs of her life (and in the nursery where Sam developed his organ of destructiveness there were ups and downs not a few); and it was the form her naughtiness took when she was [8].

"Don't care fell into a goose-pond, Miss Dot," said Nurse, on one [9] of the kind.

"I don't care if he did," said Miss Dot; and as Nurse knew no [10] feature of the goose-pond adventure which met this view of it, she closed the subject by putting Dot into the corner.

Exercise 20 - Answer Sheet:

	A	B	C	D	E	F	G	H	I
1	☐	☐	☐	☐	☐	☐	☐	☐	☐
2	☐	☐	☐	☐	☐	☐	☐	☐	☐
3	☐	☐	☐	☐	☐	☐	☐	☐	☐
4	☐	☐	☐	☐	☐	☐	☐	☐	☐
5	☐	☐	☐	☐	☐	☐	☐	☐	☐
6	☐	☐	☐	☐	☐	☐	☐	☐	☐
7	☐	☐	☐	☐	☐	☐	☐	☐	☐
8	☐	☐	☐	☐	☐	☐	☐	☐	☐
9	☐	☐	☐	☐	☐	☐	☐	☐	☐
10	☐	☐	☐	☐	☐	☐	☐	☐	☐

MULTIPLE CHOICE

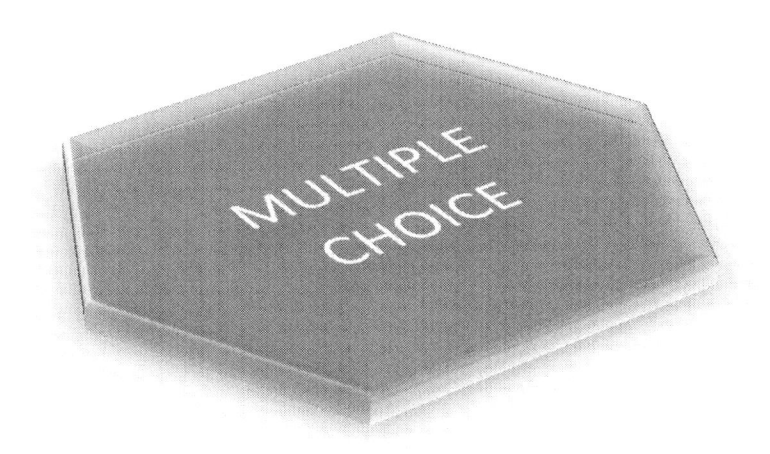

EXERCISE 21:

Instructions: For each question in the following passage, select the most appropriate word from the options given.

Marjorie sat on the door-step, shelling peas, quite unconscious what a pretty picture she made, with the roses peeping at her through the lattice work of the porch, the wind playing hide-and-seek in her (1) A. heir B. hair C. air , while the sunshine with its silent magic changed her faded gingham to a golden gown, and shimmered on the bright tin pan as if it were a silver shield. Old Rover lay at her feet, the white kitten (2) A. purred B. poured C. paired on her shoulder, and friendly robins hopped about her in the grass, chirping "A happy birthday, Marjorie!"

But the little maid neither saw nor (3) A. hard B. heard C. hear , for her eyes were fixed on the green pods, and her thoughts were far away. She was recalling the fairy-tale granny told her last night, and (4) A. screamed B. wished C. winged with all her heart that such things happened nowadays.

For in this story, as a poor girl like herself sat spinning before the door, a Brownie came by, and gave the child a good-luck penny; then a fairy passed, and left a talisman which would

keep her always happy; and last of all, the prince rolled up in his (5) A ☐ armour
B ☐ chair
C ☐ chariot ,

(6) A ☐ rein
and took her away to B ☐ rain   with him over a lovely kingdom, as a reward for
C ☐ travel

her many kindnesses to others.

When Marjorie imagined this part of the story, it was impossible to help giving one little sigh,

(7) A ☐ presents
and for a minute she forgot her work, so busy was she thinking what beautiful B ☐ prizes
C ☐ pricy

she would give to all the poor children in her realm when THEY had birthdays. Five impatient

(8) A ☐ bag
young peas took this opportunity to escape from the half-open B ☐ pod   in
C ☐ basket

her hand and skip down the steps, to be immediately gobbled up by an audacious robin, who

(9) A ☐ shook
gave thanks in such a shrill chirp that Marjorie B ☐ wake   up, laughed, and fell to
C ☐ woke

work again. She was just finishing, when a voice called out from the lane,—

"Hi, there! come here a minute, child!" and looking up, she saw a little old man in a queer

(10) A ☐ carriage
little B ☐ car   drawn by a fat little pony.
C ☐ caravan

Exercise 21 - Answer Sheet:

	A	B	C
1	☐	☐	☐
2	☐	☐	☐
3	☐	☐	☐
4	☐	☐	☐
5	☐	☐	☐
6	☐	☐	☐
7	☐	☐	☐
8	☐	☐	☐
9	☐	☐	☐
10	☐	☐	☐

EXERCISE 22:

Instructions: For each question in the following passage, select the most appropriate word from the options given.

Running down to the gate, Marjorie dropped a curtsy, saying pleasantly,—

"What did you **(1)** A ☐ wish B ☐ yell C ☐ ask , sir?"

"Just undo that check-rein for me. I am lame, and Jack wants to **(2)** A ☐ nap B ☐ eat C ☐ drink at your brook," answered the old man, nodding at her till his spectacles danced on his nose.

Marjorie was rather afraid of the fat pony, who tossed his head, whisked his tail, and stamped his feet as if he was of a **(3)** A ☐ peppery B ☐ mild C ☐ timid temper. But she liked to be useful, and just then felt as if there were few things she could NOT do if she tried, because it was her birthday. So she proudly let down the rein, and when Jack went splashing into the brook, she **(4)** A ☐ waited B ☐ went C ☐ stood on the bridge, waiting to check him up again after he had drunk his fill of the clear, cool water.

The old gentleman sat in his place, looking up at the little girl, who was smiling to herself

5 A ▢ while
B ▢ by she watched the blue dragon-flies dance among the ferns, a
C ▢ as

blackbird tilt on the alderboughs, and listened to the babble of the brook.

6 A ▢ envied
"How old are you, child?" asked the old man, as if he rather B ▢ engulfed this
C ▢ envisaged

rosy creature her youth and health.

7 A ▢ right
"Twelve to-day, sir;" and Marjorie stood up B ▢ trait and tall, as if mindful of
C ▢ straight

her years.

"Had any presents?" asked the old man, peering up with an odd smile.

8 A ▢ pushed
"One, sir,—here it is;" and she B ▢ checked out of her pocket a tin savings-
C ▢ pulled

bank in the shape of a desirable family mansion, painted red, with a green door and black

9 A ▢ Proudly
chimney. B ▢ Grumpily displaying it on the rude railing of the bridge, she
C ▢ Rudely

10 A ▢ stuff
added, with a happy face,—"Granny gave it to me, and all the B ▢ money in it
C ▢ sweets

is going to be mine."

Exercise 22 - Answer Sheet:

	A	B	C
1	☐	☐	☐
2	☐	☐	☐
3	☐	☐	☐
4	☐	☐	☐
5	☐	☐	☐
6	☐	☐	☐
7	☐	☐	☐
8	☐	☐	☐
9	☐	☐	☐
10	☐	☐	☐

EXERCISE 23:

Instructions: For each question in the following passage, select the most appropriate word from the options given.

It was a cold November storm, and everything looked forlorn. Even the pert sparrows were

draggle-tailed and too much out of spirits to
- 1 A ☐ fight
-    B ☐ yell
-    C ☐ ask

for crumbs with the fat

pigeons who tripped through the mud with their little red boots as if in haste to get back to

- 2 A ☐ nosy
their   B ☐ cozy   home in the dove-cot.
-    C ☐ noisy

But the most forlorn creature out that day was a small errand girl, with a bonnet-box on each

arm, and both hands struggling to
- 3 A ☐ drop
-    B ☐ hold
-    C ☐ held

a big broken umbrella. A pair of

worn-out boots let in the wet upon her tired feet; a thin cotton dress and an old shawl poorly

- 4 A ☐ protected
-    B ☐ purchased
-    C ☐ perceived

her from the storm; and a faded hood covered her head.

The face that looked out from this hood was too pale and anxious for one so young; and

when a sudden gust turned the old umbrella
- 5 A ☐ crash
-    B ☐ inside
-    C ☐ dampen

out with a crash, despair

fell upon poor Lizzie, and she was so miserable she could have sat down in the rain and cried.

But there was no time for tears; so, dragging the dilapidated umbrella along, she spread her

shawl over the bonnet-boxes and hurried down the broad street, eager to hide her

6
- A ☐ fortune
- B ☐ money
- C ☐ misfortunes

from a pretty young girl who stood at a window laughing at her.

She could not find the number of the house where one of the fine hats was to be left; and

after hunting all down one side of the street, she
7
- A ☐ leaned
- B ☐ crossed
- C ☐ struck

over, and came at

last to the very house where the pretty girl lived. She was no longer to be seen; and, with a

sigh of relief, Lizzie
8
- A ☐ knocked
- B ☐ rung
- C ☐ hung

the bell, and was told to wait in the hall while

Miss Belle tried the hat on.

Glad to rest, she warmed her feet, righted her
9
- A ☐ umbrella
- B ☐ Hats
- C ☐ legs

, and then sat

looking about her with eyes quick to see the beauty and the comfort that made the place so

homelike and delightful. A small waiting-room opened from the hall, and in it stood many

blooming plants, whose fragrance attracted Lizzie as irresistibly as if she had been a butterfly

or
10
- A ☐ cat
- B ☐ bee
- C ☐ bumble

.

Exercise 23 - Answer Sheet:

	A	B	C
1	▭	▭	▭
2	▭	▭	▭
3	▭	▭	▭
4	▭	▭	▭
5	▭	▭	▭
6	▭	▭	▭
7	▭	▭	▭
8	▭	▭	▭
9	▭	▭	▭
10	▭	▭	▭

EXERCISE 24:

Instructions: For each question in the following passage, select the most appropriate word from the options given.

Slipping in, she stood enjoying the lovely colors, sweet odors, and delicate shapes of these

household spirits; for Lizzie loved flowers passionately; and just then they
- 1 A ☐ perceived
- B ☐ pierced
- C ☐ possessed

a peculiar charm for her.

One particularly captivating little rose won her
- 2 A ☐ heart
- B ☐ sight
- C ☐ soul

, and made her long

for it with a longing that became a temptation too strong to resist. It was so perfect; so like a

rosy face
- 3 A ☐ smelling
- B ☐ smailing
- C ☐ turning

out from the green leaves, that Lizzie could NOT keep

her hands off it, and having smelt, touched, and kissed it, she suddenly
- 4 A ☐ pinched
- B ☐ twisted
- C ☐ broke

the stem and hid it in her pocket. Then, frightened at what she had done, she crept back to

her place in the hall, and sat there,
- 5 A ☐ burdened
- B ☐ frightened
- C ☐ angered

with remorse.

A servant came just then to lead her upstairs; for Miss Belle wished the hat altered, and must

give directions. With her heart in a flutter, and pinker roses in her cheeks than the one in her pocket, Lizzie followed to a handsome room, where a pretty girl stood before a long mirror

with the **6** A ▭ rose
         B ▭ hat   in her hand.
         C ▭ box

"Tell Madame Tifany that I don't like it at all, for she hasn't put in the blue plume mamma

ordered; and I won't have rose-buds, they are so common," said the young lady, in a

7 A ▭ dissatisfied
    B ▭ gratifying   tone, as she twirled the hat about.
    C ▭ satisfied

"Yes, miss," was all Lizzie could say; for SHE considered that hat the loveliest thing a girl

could possibly own.

"You had better ask your mamma about it, Miss Belle, before you give any orders. She will be

             8 A ▭ days
up in a few   B ▭ movements   , and the girl can wait," put in a maid, who was sewing
                 C ▭ moments

in the ante-room. "I suppose I must; but I WON'T have roses," answered Belle, crossly. Then

                                                9 A ▭ cold
she glanced at Lizzie, and said more gently, "You look very   B ▭ scared   ;
                                                     C ▭ hungry

come and sit by the fire while you wait."

                                          10 A ▭ dirty
"I'm afraid I'll wet the pretty rug, miss; my feet are   B ▭ sopping   ," said Lizzie,
                                               C ▭ soiled

gratefully, but timidly.

Exercise 24 - Answer Sheet:

	A	B	C
1	▭	▭	▭
2	▭	▭	▭
3	▭	▭	▭
4	▭	▭	▭
5	▭	▭	▭
6	▭	▭	▭
7	▭	▭	▭
8	▭	▭	▭
9	▭	▭	▭
10	▭	▭	▭

EXERCISE 25:

Instructions: For each question in the following passage, select the most appropriate word from the options given.

Belle said nothing, but sat among the sofa cushions, where she had thrown herself, looking soberly at this other girl, no older than she was, who took care of herself and was all alone in the world. It was a new idea to Belle, who was loved and petted as an only child is apt to be.

She often saw **(1)** A. roses B. girls C. beggars and pitied them, but knew very little about their wants and lives; so it was like turning a new page in her happy life to be **(2)** A. bought B. witnessing C. brought so near to poverty as this chance meeting with the milliner's girl.

"Aren't you afraid and lonely and **(3)** A. happy B. unhappy C. needy ?" she said, slowly, trying to understand and put herself in Lizzie's place.

"Yes; but it's no use. I can't help it, and may be things will get **(4)** A. affected B. worse C. better by and by, and I'll have my wish," answered Lizzie, more hopefully, because Belle's pity warmed her heart and made her troubles seem **(5)** A. heavier B. lighter C. less .

"What is your wish?" asked Belle, hoping mamma wouldn't come just yet, for she was getting interested in the stranger.

"To have a nice little room, and make flowers, like a French girl I know. It's such pretty work, and she gets lots of money, for everyone likes her

6.
A ▭ dress
B ▭ money
C ▭ flowers

. She shows me how, sometimes, and I can do leaves first-rate; but—"

There Lizzie stopped suddenly, and the color rushed up to her forehead; for she remembered the little rose in her pocket and it weighed upon her

7.
A ▭ shoulders
B ▭ mind
C ▭ conscience

like a stone.

Before Belle could ask what was the matter, Marie came in with a tray of cake and fruit,

saying: "Here's your lunch, Miss Belle."

"Put it down, please; I'm not ready for it yet."

And Belle shook her head as she glanced at Lizzie, who was staring hard at the fire with such a troubled face that Belle could not

8.
A ▭ bear
B ▭ afford
C ▭ bare

to see it. Jumping out of her nest

9.
A ▭ roses
of B ▭ plates
C ▭ cushions

, she heaped a plate with good things, and going to Lizzie, offered it, saying, with a gentle

10.
A ▭ curiosity
B ▭ courtesy
C ▭ cure

that made the act doubly

sweet: "Please have some; you must be tired of waiting."

Exercise 25 - Answer Sheet:

	A	B	C
1	☐	☐	☐
2	☐	☐	☐
3	☐	☐	☐
4	☐	☐	☐
5	☐	☐	☐
6	☐	☐	☐
7	☐	☐	☐
8	☐	☐	☐
9	☐	☐	☐
10	☐	☐	☐

EXERCISE 26:

Instructions: For each question in the following passage, select the most appropriate word from the options given.

But Lizzie could not take it; she could only cover her face and cry; for this kindness rent her heart and made the stolen flower a burden too heavy to be

1
- A ▢ borne
- B ▢ carry
- C ▢ felt

.

"Oh, don't cry so! Are you sick? Have I been rude? Tell me all about it; and if I can't do anything, mamma can," said Belle, surprised and

2
- A ▢ troubled
- B ▢ happy
- C ▢ scared

.

"No; I'm not sick; I'm bad, and I can't bear it when you are so good to me," sobbed Lizzie, quite overcome with penitence; and taking out the crumpled rose, she

3
- A ▢ confiscated
- B ▢ confessed
- C ▢ carried

her fault with many tears.

"Don't feel so much about such a little thing as that," began Belle, warmly; then checked herself, and added, more soberly, "It WAS

4
- A ▢ wrong
- B ▢ okay
- C ▢ just

to take it without leave; but it's all right now, and I'll give you as many roses as you want, for I know you are a good girl."

"Thank you. I didn't want it only because it was pretty,

5
- A ▢ as
- B ▢ since
- C ▢ but

I wanted to copy it. I can't get any for myself, and so I can't do my make-believe ones well. Madame won't even lend me the old ones in the store, and Estelle has none to spare for me, because I

can't pay her for (6) A ☐ preaching
              B ☐ ruining   me. She gives me bits of muslin and wire and
              C ☐ teaching

things, and shows me now and then. But I know if I had a real flower I could copy it; so she'd

see I did know something, for I try real hard. I'm SO tired of (7) A ☐ slopping
                                                                  B ☐ waking   round
                                                                  C ☐ making

the streets; I'd do anything to earn my living some other way."

Lizzie had poured out her trouble rapidly; and the little story was quite affecting when one

saw the tears on her (8) A ☐ eyes
                          B ☐ cheeks   , the poor clothes, and the thin hands that held
                          C ☐ life

the stolen rose. Belle was much touched, and, in her impetuous way, set about mending

(9) A ☐ boots
    B ☐ matters   as fast as possible.
    C ☐ flowers

"Put on those boots and that pair of dry stockings right away. Then tuck as much cake and

fruit into your pocket as it will hold. I'm going to get you some flowers, and see if mamma is

              (10) A ☐ abscond
too busy to   B ☐ cheeks   to me." With a nod and a smile, Belle flew about the
                   C ☐ attend

room a minute; then vanished, leaving Lizzie to her comfortable task, feeling as if fairies still

haunted the world as in the good old times.

Exercise 26 - Answer Sheet:

	A	B	C
1	☐	☐	☐
2	☐	☐	☐
3	☐	☐	☐
4	☐	☐	☐
5	☐	☐	☐
6	☐	☐	☐
7	☐	☐	☐
8	☐	☐	☐
9	☐	☐	☐
10	☐	☐	☐

EXERCISE 27:

Instructions: For each question in the following passage, select the most appropriate word from the options given.

When Belle came back with a handful of roses, she found Lizzie

1.
- A ☐ absorbed
- B ☐ observed
- C ☐ disgusted

in admiring contemplation of her new boots, as she ate sponge-cake in a blissful sort of waking-dream.

"Mamma can't come; but I don't care about the hat. It will do very well, and isn't worth

2.
- A ☐ fuming
- B ☐ fussing
- C ☐ fighting

about. There, will those be of any use to you?" And she offered the nosegay with a much happier face than the one Lizzie first saw.

"Oh, miss, they're just lovely! I'll copy that pink rose as soon as ever I can, and when I've

3.
- A ☐ bound
- B ☐ tucked
- C ☐ learned

to do 'em tip-top, I'd like to bring you some, if you don't mind,"

answered Lizzie, smiling all over her face as she

4.
- A ☐ smelled
- B ☐ buried
- C ☐ struck

her nose luxuriously in the fragrant mass.

"I'd like it very much, for I should think you'd have to be very clever to make such pretty things. I really quite fancy those rosebuds in my hat, now I know that you're going to learn how to make them. Put an orange in your pocket, and the flowers in (5) A. bunch B. water C. stream as soon as you can, so they'll be fresh when you want them. Good-by. Bring home our hats every time and tell me how you get on."

With kind words like these, Belle dismissed Lizzie, who ran downstairs, feeling as rich as if she had found a (6) A. bunch B. fortress C. fortune . Away to the next place she hurried, anxious to get her errands done and the precious posy safely into fresh water. But Mrs. Turretviile was not at home, and the bonnet could not be left till paid for. So Lizzie turned to go down the high steps, glad that she need not (7) A. wait B. weight C. wear . She stopped one instant to take a delicious sniff at her flowers, and that was the last happy moment that poor Lizzie knew for many (8) A. weary B. wary C. bright months.

The new boots were large for her, the steps (9) A. wet B. slippery C. dry with sleet, and down went the little errand girl, from top to bottom, till she landed in the gutter directly upon Mrs. Turretville's costly bonnet. "I've (10) A. lost B. messed C. saved my posies, anyway," sighed Lizzie, as she picked herself up, bruised, wet, and faint with pain.

Exercise 27 - Answer Sheet:

	A	B	C
1	☐	☐	☐
2	☐	☐	☐
3	☐	☐	☐
4	☐	☐	☐
5	☐	☐	☐
6	☐	☐	☐
7	☐	☐	☐
8	☐	☐	☐
9	☐	☐	☐
10	☐	☐	☐

EXERCISE 28:

Instructions: For each question in the following passage, select the most appropriate word from the options given.

'If anyone had told me what wonderful changes were to take place here in ten years, I wouldn't have believed it,' said Mrs Jo to Mrs Meg, as they sat on the piazza at Plumfield one summer day, looking about them with faces full of pride and

1. A ☐ pressure
   B ☐ pleasure
   C ☐ disgrace

'This is the sort of magic that money and kind hearts can work. I am sure Mr Laurence could have no nobler

2. A ☐ monument
   B ☐ dwelling
   C ☐ montage

than the college he so generously endowed; and a home like this will keep Aunt March's memory

3. A ☐ green
   B ☐ red
   C ☐ amber

as long as it lasts,' answered Mrs Meg, always glad to praise the absent.

'We used to believe in fairies, you remember, and plan what we'd ask for if we could have three

4. A ☐ wonders
   B ☐ dreams
   C ☐ wishes

. Doesn't it seem as if mine had been really granted at last? Money, fame, and plenty of the work I love,' said Mrs Jo, carelessly rumpling up her hair as she

5. A ☐ clapped
   B ☐ cobbled
   C ☐ clasped

her hands over her head just as she used to do when a girl.

'I have had mine, and Amy is enjoying hers to her heart's content. If dear Marmee, John, and

(6) A ☐ quiet
Beth were here, it would be B ☐ quite   perfect,' added Meg, with a tender
C ☐ quit

quiver in her voice; for Marmee's place was empty now.

Jo put her hand on her sister's, and both sat silent for a little while, surveying the pleasant

(7) A ☐ mingled
scene before them with B ☐ minced   sad and happy thoughts.
C ☐ hewn

It certainly did look as if magic had been at work, for quiet Plumfield was transformed into a

(8) A ☐ hospital
busy little world. The house seemed more B ☐ hostile   than ever, refreshed now
C ☐ hospitable

with new paint, added wings, well-kept lawn and garden, and a prosperous air it had not

worn when riotous boys swarmed everywhere and it was rather difficult for the Bhaers to

(9) A ☐ kites
make both ends meet. On the hill, where B ☐ butterflies   used to be flown, stood
C ☐ bees

the fine college which Mr Laurence's munificent legacy had built. Busy students were going

to and fro along the paths once trodden by childish feet, and many young men and women

(10) A ☐ advantages
were enjoying all the B ☐ hardships   that wealth, wisdom, and benevolence could
C ☐ drawbacks

give them.

Exercise 28 - Answer Sheet:

	A	B	C
1	▭	▭	▭
2	▭	▭	▭
3	▭	▭	▭
4	▭	▭	▭
5	▭	▭	▭
6	▭	▭	▭
7	▭	▭	▭
8	▭	▭	▭
9	▭	▭	▭
10	▭	▭	▭

EXERCISE 29:

Instructions: For each question in the following passage, select the most appropriate word from the options given.

It was well named; and the Muses seemed to be at home that day, for as the newcomers went up the

1. A ☐ slope
   B ☐ slip
   C ☐ road

appropriate sights and sounds greeted them. Passing an window, they looked in upon a library presided over by Clio, Calliope, and Urania; Melpomene and Thalia were disporting themselves in the hall, where some young people were dancing and rehearsing a play; Erato was walking in the garden with her lover, and in the music-room Phoebus himself was drilling a tuneful

2. A ☐ tune
   B ☐ choir
   C ☐ memoir

A mature Apollo was our old friend Laurie, but comely and genial as ever; for time had

3. A ☐ ripped
   B ☐ strewn
   C ☐ ripened

the freakish boy into a noble man. Care and sorrow, as well as ease and happiness, had done much for him; and the

4. A ☐ responsibility
   B ☐ accountability
   C ☐ respite

carrying out his grandfather's wishes had been a duty most faithfully performed. Prosperity suits some people, and they blossom best in a glow of sunshine; others need the shade, and are the sweeter for a touch of frost. Laurie was one of the former sort, and Amy was another; so

life had been a kind of poem to them since they married—not only
5
- A ☐ harmonious
- B ☐ hampered
- C ☐ harmful

and happy, but earnest, useful, and rich in the beautiful benevolence which can do so much

when wealth and wisdom go hand in hand with charity. Their house was full of

unostentatious beauty and
6
- A ☐ comfort
- B ☐ beast
- C ☐ filth

, and here the art-loving host and hostess

attracted and entertained artists of all kinds. Laurie had music enough now, and was a

generous patron to the class he most liked to help. Amy had her proteges among ambitious

young painters and sculptors, and
7
- A ☐ found
- B ☐ founded
- C ☐ frowned

her own art double dear as her

daughter grew old enough to share its labours and delights with her; for she was one of

those who prove that
8
- A ☐ people
- B ☐ men
- C ☐ women

can be faithful wives and without sacrificing the

special gift bestowed upon them for their own development and the
9
- A ☐ good
- B ☐ evolve
- C ☐ evil
of

others. Her sisters
10
- A ☐ new
- B ☐ known
- C ☐ knew

where to find her.

Exercise 29 - Answer Sheet:

	A	B	C
1	☐	☐	☐
2	☐	☐	☐
3	☐	☐	☐
4	☐	☐	☐
5	☐	☐	☐
6	☐	☐	☐
7	☐	☐	☐
8	☐	☐	☐
9	☐	☐	☐
10	☐	☐	☐

EXERCISE 30:

Instructions: For each question in the following passage, select the most appropriate word from the options given.

It was evident that she **(1)** A ☐ adorned / B ☐ adored / C ☐ adjudged her daughter, and well she might; for the beauty she had longed for seemed, to her fond eyes at least, to be impersonated in this younger self. Bess **(2)** A ☐ inherited / B ☐ indebted / C ☐ endangered her mother's Diana-like figure, blue eyes, fair skin, and golden hair, tied up in the same classic knot of curls. Also—ah! never-ending source of joy to Amy—she had her father's handsome nose and mouth, cast in a feminine mould.

The severe simplicity of a long linen pinafore **(3)** A ☐ belittled / B ☐ struck / C ☐ suited her; and she worked away with the entire absorption of the true artist, unconscious of the loving eyes upon her, till Aunt Jo came in **(4)** A ☐ exclaiming / B ☐ piercing / C ☐ exhausted eagerly:

'My dear girls, stop your mud-pies and hear the news!'

Both artists dropped their tools and greeted the **(5)** A ☐ Irrepressible / B ☐ calm / C ☐ timid woman cordially, though genius had been burning splendidly and her coming spoilt a precious hour. They were in the full tide of gossip when Laurie, who had been summoned by Meg, arrived, and sitting

down **6** A ☐ between
      B ☐ above   the sisters, with no barricade anywhere, listened with interest
      C ☐ over

to the news of Franz and Emil.

'The epidemic has broke out, and now it will rage and ravage your flock. Be **7** A ☐ prepared
                                                                                B ☐ nervous
                                                                                C ☐ calm

for every sort of romance and rashness for the next ten years, Jo. Your boys are growing up

and will plunge headlong into a sea of worse scrapes than any you have had yet,' said Laurie,

enjoying her look of mingled delight and **8** A ☐ despair
                                              B ☐ above
                                              C ☐ joy

'I know it, and I hope I shall be able to pull them through and land them safely; but it's an

awful responsibility, for they will come to me and **9** A ☐ refute
                                                         B ☐ reject   that I can make
                                                         C ☐ insist

their poor little loves run smoothly. I like it, though, and Meg is such a mush of sentiment she

revels in the prospect,' answered Jo, **10** A ☐ feeling
                                              B ☐ screaming pretty easy about her own boys,
                                              C ☐ seeking

whose youth made them safe for the present.

Exercise 30 - Answer Sheet:

	A	B	C
1	☐	☐	☐
2	☐	☐	☐
3	☐	☐	☐
4	☐	☐	☐
5	☐	☐	☐
6	☐	☐	☐
7	☐	☐	☐
8	☐	☐	☐
9	☐	☐	☐
10	☐	☐	☐

ANSWERS

ANSWERS:

EXERCISE 1 Cloze		EXERCISE 2 Cloze		EXERCISE 3 Cloze		EXERCISE 4 Cloze		EXERCISE 5 Cloze	
1	H	1	H	1	F	1	H	1	H
2	D	2	A	2	A	2	C	2	A
3	A	3	F	3	H	3	A	3	I
4	J	4	E	4	J	4	J	4	B
5	B	5	I	5	I	5	E	5	D
6	F	6	B	6	E	6	D	6	G
7	C	7	D	7	D	7	B	7	E
8	I	8	G	8	B	8	F	8	C
9	G	9	C	9	C	9	I	9	J
10	E	10	J	10	G	10	G	10	F

ANSWERS:

EXERCISE 6 Cloze		EXERCISE 7 Cloze		EXERCISE 8 Cloze		EXERCISE 9 Cloze		EXERCISE 10 Cloze	
1	B	1	B	1	A	1	B	1	A
2	I	2	H	2	F	2	F	2	H
3	J	3	A	3	C	3	H	3	F
4	E	4	D	4	H	4	A	4	I
5	D	5	J	5	B	5	J	5	D
6	A	6	C	6	G	6	C	6	C
7	F	7	E	7	D	7	I	7	G
8	G	8	F	8	E	8	D	8	J
9	C	9	G	9	J	9	E	9	E
10	H	10	I	10	I	10	G	10	B

ANSWERS:

EXERCISE 11 Cloze		EXERCISE 12 Cloze		EXERCISE 13 Cloze		EXERCISE 14 Cloze		EXERCISE 15 Cloze	
1	H	1	F	1	A	1	G	1	D
2	A	2	B	2	H	2	F	2	A
3	J	3	J	3	F	3	J	3	G
4	D	4	A	4	B	4	A	4	B
5	G	5	H	5	D	5	H	5	F
6	E	6	C	6	E	6	D	6	C
7	C	7	G	7	J	7	C	7	J
8	I	8	E	8	G	8	I	8	E
9	F	9	D	9	I	9	B	9	H
10	B	10	I	10	C	10	E	10	I

ANSWERS:

EXERCISE 16 Cloze		EXERCISE 17 Cloze		EXERCISE 18 Cloze		EXERCISE 19 Cloze		EXERCISE 20 Cloze	
1	F	1	C	1	G	1	E	1	G
2	B	2	A	2	A	2	A	2	A
3	A	3	G	3	B	3	G	3	F
4	J	4	E	4	I	4	J	4	D
5	H	5	I	5	C	5	C	5	J
6	D	6	J	6	D	6	B	6	B
7	G	7	B	7	J	7	F	7	C
8	E	8	H	8	F	8	I	8	I
9	C	9	D	9	H	9	D	9	H
10	I	10	F	10	E	10	H	10	E

ANSWERS:

EXERCISE 21 Cloze		EXERCISE 22 Cloze		EXERCISE 23 Cloze		EXERCISE 24 Cloze		EXERCISE 25 Cloze	
1	B	1	A	1	A	1	C	1	C
2	A	2	C	2	B	2	A	2	C
3	B	3	A	3	B	3	B	3	B
4	B	4	C	4	A	4	C	4	C
5	C	5	C	5	B	5	A	5	B
6	A	6	A	6	C	6	B	6	C
7	A	7	C	7	B	7	A	7	C
8	B	8	C	8	B	8	C	8	C
9	C	9	A	9	A	9	A	9	C
10	A	10	B	10	B	10	B	10	B

ANSWERS:

EXERCISE 26 Cloze		EXERCISE 27 Cloze		EXERCISE 28 Cloze		EXERCISE 29 Cloze		EXERCISE 30 Cloze	
1	A	1	A	1	B	1	A	1	B
2	A	2	B	2	A	2	B	2	A
3	B	3	C	3	A	3	C	3	C
4	A	4	B	4	C	4	A	4	A
5	C	5	B	5	C	5	A	5	A
6	C	6	C	6	B	6	A	6	A
7	A	7	A	7	A	7	A	7	A
8	B	8	A	8	C	8	C	8	A
9	B	9	B	9	A	9	A	9	C
10	C	10	C	10	A	10	C	10	A

Other books in the **Mastering 11+** series:

- English & Verbal Reasoning – Practice Book 1
- English & Verbal Reasoning – Practice Book 2
- English & Verbal Reasoning – Practice Book 3

- Cloze Tests – Practice Book 2
- Cloze Tests – Practice Book 3

- Maths – Practice Book 1
- Maths – Practice Book 2
- Maths – Practice Book 3

- Comprehension – Multiple Choice Exercise Book 1
- Comprehension – Multiple Choice Exercise Book 2
- Comprehension – Multiple Choice Exercise Book 3

- CEM Practice Papers – Pack 1
- CEM Practice Papers – Pack 2
- CEM Practice Papers – Pack 3
- CEM Practice Papers – Pack 4

All queries to **enquiry@mastering11plus.com**

Printed in Great Britain
by Amazon.co.uk, Ltd.,
Marston Gate.